Country File
Bangladesh

Michael March

FRANKLIN WATTS
LONDON • SYDNEY

Revised and updated 2006

Franklin Watts
338 Euston Road, London
NW1 3BH

Franklin Watts Australia
Hachette Children's Books
Level 17/207 Kent Street
Sydney NSW 2000

COUNTRY FILE: BANGLADESH produced for Franklin Watts
by Bender Richardson White, PO Box 266, Uxbridge, UK.
Editor: Lionel Bender
Designer and Page Make-up: Ben White
Picture Researcher: Cathy Stastny
Cover Make-up: Mike Pilley, Radius
Production: Kim Richardson

Graphics and Maps: Stefan Chabluk

Consultant: Dr Terry Jennings, a former geography teacher
and university lecturer. He is now a full-time writer of
children's geography and science books.

A CIP catalogue record for this book is available
from the British Library.

ISBN 0 7496 6654 4

Dewey Classification: 915.492

Printed in China

Picture Credits

Pages 1: Corbis Images/Roger Wood. 3: James Davis Travel
Photography. 4: Robert Harding/Liba Taylor.
7: Hutchison/Liba Taylor. 8: Hutchison/Dirk. R. Frans.
9, 11: Hutchison/Liba Taylor. 12–13: James Davis Travel
Photography. 14: Hutchison/Dirk R. Frans. 15: James
Davis Travel Photography. 17 top: Hutchison/Dirk R.
Frans. 17 bottom: Hutchison/Liba Taylor. 18: Robert
Harding Photo Library. 19: Hutchison/Liba Taylor. 20:
Panos Pictures/Zed Nelson. 21: Hutchison Library.
22–23: Robert Harding/Liba Taylor. 23: Hutchison/Trevor
Page. 24: Hutchison/Bruce Wills. 25: Corbis Images/
Roger Wood. 26–27: James Davis Travel Photography.
28: Robert Harding/Nigel Cromm. 30: Hutchison/Dirk
R. Frans. 31: Hutchison Library.

Cover Photo: Hutchison Library/Dirk R. Frans.

The Author

Michael March is a full-time writer and
editor of non-fiction books. He has
written more than 20 books for children
about different countries of the world.

Note to parents and teachers

Every effort has been made by the Publishers to ensure
that the websites in this book are suitable for children,
that they are of the highest educational value, and that
they contain no inappropriate or offensive material.
However, because of the nature of the Internet, it is
impossible to guarantee that the contents of these sites
will not be altered. We strongly advise that Internet
access is supervised by a responsible adult.

Contents

Welcome to Bangladesh

The People's Republic of Bangladesh is a country on the Indian subcontinent, in southern Asia. It occupies some 147,000 square kilometres, making it about the size of England and Wales put together, or of the state of Illinois in the USA. The terrain is mostly flat, low-lying and subject to flooding.

The name Bangladesh means 'land of the Bengali people' in the Bengali language. Some Bengalis also live across the border in India, in the state of West Bengal. The Bengalis are an ancient people, with a history going back thousands of years. But Bangladesh as an independent country is only some 30 years old. Before 1971, it was a division of India's great rival, Pakistan.

Bangladeshis are famous for their handicrafts. The finely woven cotton muslin from Dhaka has been prized since the time of the ancient Romans. Other traditional Bangladeshi products include pink pearls, embroidered silk robes, called *sarees*, and delicate silver filigree jewellery.

DATABASE

Neighbours

Bangladesh shares its western, northern and eastern borders with its huge neighbour, India. The southern boundary is a 580-kilometre stretch of coastline washed by the waters of the Bay of Bengal. To the south-east lies the country called Myanmar, or Burma.

The capital city, Dhaka – formerly spelled Dacca – is a crowded, sprawling mass of buildings. ▼

NEPAL

BHUTAN

26°N

N
W E
S

Mountains ▲ Mountain peak
Grassland and farming
□ Capital ○ Major city
Country boundary

0   100 Miles

0   100 Kilometres

○ Rangpur

○ Dinajpur

○ Bogra   Jamālpur ○   25°N

Brahmaputra (Jamuna) River

○ Mymensingh

○ Sylhet

Kalni River

○ Rajshahi

Ganges (Ganga) River

INDIA

BANGLADESH

Brahmanbāria ○

24°N

□ DHAKA

Comilla ○

Tropic of
Cancer

Jessore ○

Haringhat River

CHITTAGONG HILLS

Chandpur ○

23°N

INDIA

Khulna ○

Bagherhat ○

Barisal ○

GANGES   DELTA

Mongla Port ○

Chittagong ○

Tahjindong △

S U N D A R B A N S

Sangu River

22°N

Bay of Bengal

MYANMAR

21°N

88°E   89°E   90°E   91°E   92°E

The Land

Plants and Animals

Acacia and banyan trees grow in the drier lowland areas. Broadleaf, evergreen and garyan trees are found in the Chittagong Hills, which are home to elephants and leopards. The Sundarbans, in the south-west, is the world's largest mangrove forest, and the habitat of the Bengal tiger. Altogether, Bangladesh has some 200 species of mammals, 120 species of reptiles, 700 species of birds and 200 species of fish.

Much of Bangladesh is made up of the lowland delta region of the Padma (or Ganges) and Jamuna (or Brahmaputra) rivers. Here, on the floodplain, at the head of the Bay of Bengal, silt deposited by frequent flooding of rivers and the sea has created some of the world's most fertile soil.

Only about 10 per cent of Bangladesh is hilly. Most of the hills are between 600 and 900 metres high, and are in Chittagong province, in the south-east. Forests grow on some slopes, but many forests have been cleared. The highest peak is Tahjindong (1,412 metres), in Barnadang province, which borders on Myanmar.

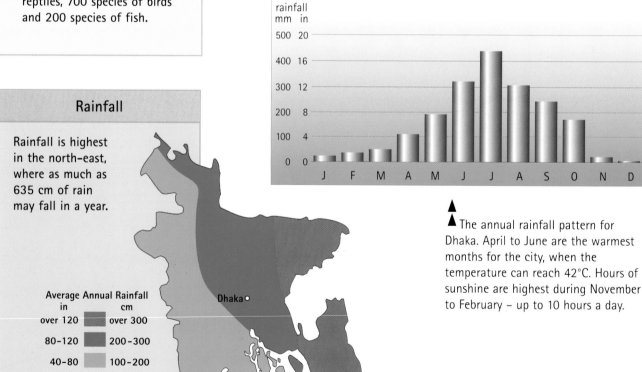

▲ The annual rainfall pattern for Dhaka. April to June are the warmest months for the city, when the temperature can reach 42°C. Hours of sunshine are highest during November to February – up to 10 hours a day.

Rainfall

Rainfall is highest in the north-east, where as much as 635 cm of rain may fall in a year.

Average Annual Rainfall	
in	cm
over 120	over 300
80–120	200–300
40–80	100–200

Dhaka○

Climate

In Bangladesh, it is warm and humid year round, and temperatures do not vary greatly from region to region. The east of the country gets, on average, about three times as much rain as the west. About 80 per cent of all the rain falls between May and September, during the monsoon, when some 30 per cent of the country becomes flooded. During the drier months, some parts of the country experience droughts.

Floods

At the beginning and end of the monsoon season, cyclones – violent tropical rainstorms with high winds – can well up in the Bay of Bengal. A powerful cyclone can rip through towns and villages on the shore and cause huge waves, flooding coastal areas. In 1970, a cyclone in Bangladesh killed some 500,000 people, and another in 1991 cost 120,000 lives and left millions of people homeless.

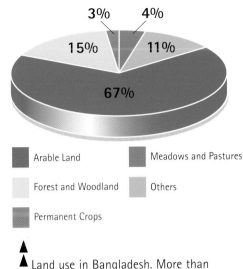

3% 4%
15% 11%
67%

Arable Land   Meadows and Pastures

Forest and Woodland   Others

Permanent Crops

Land use in Bangladesh. More than 80 per cent of the land is used for agriculture and forestry.

Thatched- or corrugated iron-roofed houses are scattered across the countryside. Roads and houses are raised above the ground to avoid damage from flooding. ▼

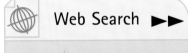

Web Search ►►

► http://www.bangladesh online.com/bmd/
The official Bangladesh Meteorological Department's website, including data on the country's climate and satellite weather maps.

► http://www.bssnews.net/ about_bangladesh.php
Bangladesh Bureau of Statistics news site, with information on climate, plants, animals and other topics.

► http://www.discovery bangladesh.com/dream_ dest_chittagong.html
Tourist site with page on Chittagong town and Chittagong district.

The People

Bangladesh has some 144 million people, making it the world's seventh-largest country in terms of population. About 98 per cent of Bangladeshi people are ethnic Bengalis. The rest belong to more than thirty other ethnic groups, who have their own traditions and their own cultures.

Bengalis have their roots in peoples who, thousands of years ago, migrated from the regions that are today Myanmar, northern India, and Tibet in China. These peoples settled the area that is now Bangladesh. They mixed and bred with the local people of different races and religions that they found there.

The main street of Bhola, a town of about 50,000 people in the south of Bangladesh. The street is crowded with rickshaws. ▼

Language

The official language of Bangladesh is Bangla, which is also called Bengali and is spoken by all Bengalis. It is based on an ancient language called Sanskrit, and written using a script derived from it.

Like Bengali, English is also widely used in Bangladesh. Many of the people who migrated here from India in the late 1940s also speak and write in the Urdu language. Some of the languages spoken in the south-east of the country are similar to Burmese, the language of Myanmar.

▲▲ Ethnic Bengalis tend to have dark skin and black hair and be of medium height and build.

A comparison of the percentage of Bangladeshi males and females of all ages. ▶▶

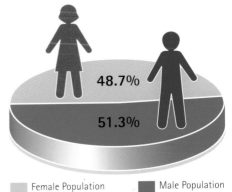

48.7%

51.3%

Female Population
70,313,914

Male Population
74,005,714

Tribes and ethnic groups

The ethnic minorities of Bangladesh include hill-tribes, such as the Chakmas and Moghs, who live in the forests of the Chittagong Hills and are descended from the Mongols of central Asia. Other ethnic groups, such as the Santal and Biharis, arrived in the 1940s, from India.

Age groups

Bangladesh is a young country, with more than a third of the population under 15 years of age and a half under 25. Only some 3 per cent of the people are 65 or older. Boys outnumber girls, and men outnumber women, in every age group. Proportionally, the biggest difference between the sexes is in the over 65s, where there are about 10 per cent more men than women. Overall, Bangladeshi males outnumber females by 5 per cent. Fifty years ago, this difference was nearly 10 per cent.

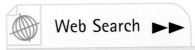

Web Search ▶▶

▶ http://www.discovery
bangladesh.com/meet
bangladesh/statistic.html
Population statistics from website describing itself as the 'First Travel and Tourist Portal of Bangladesh'.

▶ http://www.bbsgov.org/
Data on people from the Bangladesh Bureau of Statistics.

Urban and Rural Life

On average, about 985 people live on every square kilometre of Bangladesh. It is one of the most densely populated countries on Earth. About three-quarters of the people live in rural areas, but this proportion is decreasing, as more people move to the towns and cities. The total population is growing by about 2.1 per cent a year.

With some 9 million people, Dhaka, the country's capital, is by far the biggest city. Next biggest is Chittagong, a major port town with a population of some 3.7 million. Farther east, the Chittagong Hills, which are home to some of the ethnic minority groups, have fewer people than most other areas. The most sparsely populated region is the Sundarbans, the swampy mangrove forest by the south-west coast, where there are only about 30 people per square kilometre.

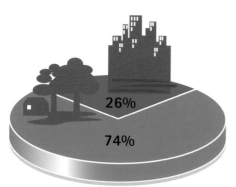

26%

74%

■ Percentage of Population Living in Urban Areas

■ Percentage of Population Living in Rural Areas

In recent years, there has been a repeated annual increase in urban population of about 4 per cent.

Clothing

Men in towns usually wear shirts and trousers, shoes and socks, as in the West. In rural areas, men wear the traditional Begali *lungi*, a kind of skirt, and often go barefoot. Most Bengali women wear the traditional *saree*, a wide strip of cotton or silk that is wrapped round the body and draped over one shoulder.

Population

Due to the high population density, overcrowding is a problem in most cities and in many rural areas.

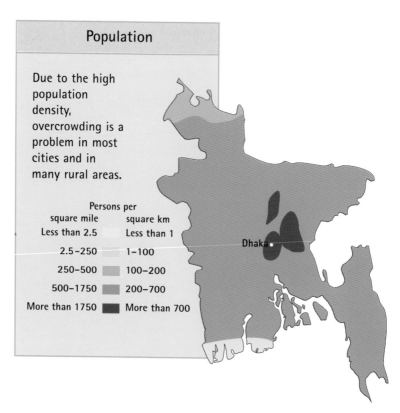

Persons per	
square mile	square km
Less than 2.5	Less than 1
2.5–250	1–100
250–500	100–200
500–1750	200–700
More than 1750	More than 700

Dhaka

Houses and homes

In the countryside, villagers build their houses of bamboo with a thatched or metal roof. The houses are usually small, with one or two rooms for a family, and some have no electricity. In times of serious flooding, people build platforms, raised above the water on bamboo poles, or move on to the roof or live in small boats.

In the towns and cities, some families have brick or concrete homes or live in small apartment buildings. But many live crowded together in small wooden houses. In the poorest districts, houses are made of sticks, scraps of wood or cardboard.

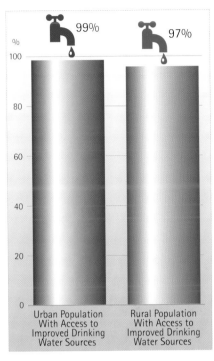

In rural areas most people get their drinking water from public standpipes, wells, boreholes or protected springs. ▼

Almost everyone has access to improved drinking water sources but only a small proportion of houses have modern plumbing. ▶▶

🌐 Web Search ▶▶

► http://www.discovery bangladesh.com/meet bangladesh/demo graphic_feature.html
Population distribution and other human geography information.

► http://www.world-gazetteer.com/fr/ fr_bd.htm
Populations for cities, towns and regions of Bangladesh.

► http://www.bangladesh online.com/tourism/ popu.htm
Page on population accessed through Bangladesh Online, an Internet service provider.

Farming and Fishing

Well over half of the working people of Bangladesh work on the land. Most of them are rice farmers. Rice and fish make up the major part of the nation's diet. Fish, along with shellfish, are taken from the sea or rivers, or are raised in ponds.

Bangladesh has some 17 million farmers. Many of these farm small plots of land (average size 1.5 hectares), using hand tools and such animals as bullocks to do the work. Some farms have now formed cooperatives, and are sharing farm machinery.

Farm produce accounts for about one-fifth of Bangladesh's gross domestic product – a measure of the country's economic activity. In many areas, rice, the major crop, can be harvested three times in the year. After rice, wheat is the second most important cereal crop. The main cash crop – the main crop grown for export – is jute, which is used to make rope and mats. Bangladesh is the world's largest producer of jute. Another major cash crop is tea.

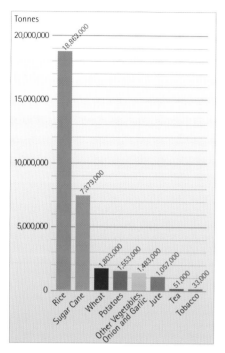

▲▲ Comparative production of crops by weight.

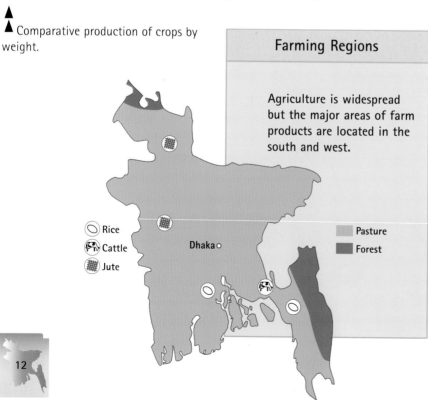

Farming Regions

Agriculture is widespread but the major areas of farm products are located in the south and west.

Dhaka○

◯ Rice
🐂 Cattle
▦ Jute

▦ Pasture
▦ Forest

Fruit and animals

Bangladeshi farmers also grow sugar cane and vegetables as well as a wide variety of fruit, including jack fruit, mangoes and bananas. Cattle are kept mainly for their skins, rather than for meat, and animal hides are an important export product.

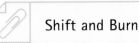

Shift and Burn

Some Bangladeshi hill-tribes still farm by the ancient 'shift and burn' method. They clear an area for cultivation by cutting down trees and burning them along with the grass, and use the ashes as fertilizer. They then sow the seeds and harvest the crop, before moving on to another patch, leaving the abandoned patch to return to grass or forest.

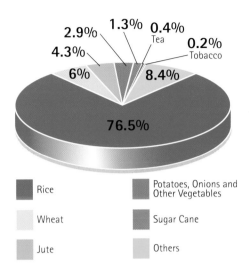

2.9% 1.3% 0.4% Tea 0.2% Tobacco
4.3%
6% 8.4%
76.5%

- Rice
- Wheat
- Jute
- Potatoes, Onions and Other Vegetables
- Sugar Cane
- Others

Fish and shellfish

Over a million Bangladeshis fish for a living. Many more involve themselves in fishing during the monsoon season. Some 70 trawlers along with 5,000 smaller, powered boats and more than a million traditional, non-powered fishing boats make up the nation's fishing fleet. Hilsa, a kind of herring, and prawns, are a major part of the catch. Prawns are also farmed in special ponds for export. Catfish, carp and other varieties are fished in the country's many rivers.

▲ Of all crops, rice is produced in the highest quantity, but minor crops such as tea and tobacco are very important as exports.

Web Search ►►

► http://www.bbsgov.org/
Official production figures from Bangladesh Bureau of Statistics.

► http://www.sdnbd.org/ sdi/metadata/bangladesh _data_profile.htm
Data profile of Bangladesh on website of Sustainable Development Networking Project.

► http://www.fao.org/fi/ statist/summtab/default. asp
World fishing figures on United Nations Food and Agriculture Organization website.

◄◄ Fishermen unload their catch of freshwater fish from small boats on a riverbank in Dhaka.

Resources and Industry

DATABASE

Cheap labour

Many factories produce clothing and knitwear, which are major export items. Hundreds of thousands of bales of cotton are imported each year and made into cloth for the clothing industry or for sale as textiles. Other factories turn jute into burlap (for making sacks), or make leather goods and steel. Service industries include banking, transport, hotels and catering. Labour is cheap in Bangladesh. Many workers are paid the equivalent of under £1 a day.

Industrial workers make up a little over one-tenth of the Bangladeshi workforce, but they create nearly one-fifth of the country's wealth. About one-quarter of the working population are service-sector workers, who contribute more than a half of the nation's gross domestic product (a measure of wealth). Much of the country's energy is supplied by natural gas.

Bangladesh has more than twenty gas fields, some of them offshore and some not yet fully operational. Coal is mined in Rajshahi division, in the north-west. Between them, natural gas and coal account for more than 90 per cent of the country's annual electricity output. The rest comes mainly from HEP (hydro-electric power) generated by dams on rivers, such as the Sangu and Matamuhuri, in the Chittagong Hills region.

Sewing clothes in a garment factory. ▼
▼

Output by weight for major manufactured goods. ▶▶

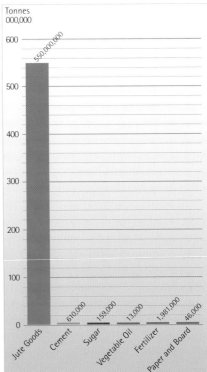

Tonnes 000,000

Jute Goods	550,000,000
Cement	610,000
Sugar	159,000
Vegetable Oil	13,000
Fertilizer	1,981,000
Paper and Board	46,000

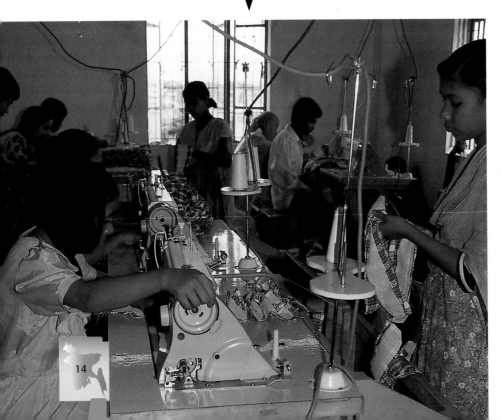

14

Resources and reserves

About half of the fuel used in homes for heating and cooking is from traditional sources, such as wood, animal dung or crop waste. Other energy needs are met by oil, most of it imported, as Bangladesh possesses only small oil reserves.

The high methane content of the natural gas makes it ideal for producing fertilizer, which is one the country's leading products. Sand, found in quantities in Bangladesh, is used in glassmaking. Local limestone and hard rock provide cement and other building materials for the construction industry. Bamboo is pulped to make paper.

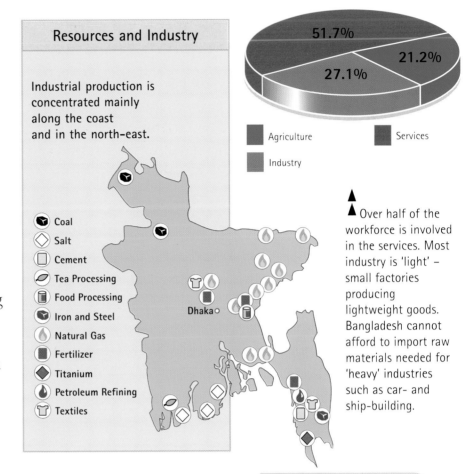

Resources and Industry

Industrial production is concentrated mainly along the coast and in the north-east.

- 🐦 Coal
- ◇ Salt
- ▯ Cement
- 🍃 Tea Processing
- 🥫 Food Processing
- ⚙ Iron and Steel
- 💧 Natural Gas
- ▪ Fertilizer
- ◆ Titanium
- 💧 Petroleum Refining
- ⊕ Textiles

Dhaka ○

- 51.7%
- 21.2%
- 27.1%

■ Agriculture   ■ Services
■ Industry

▲ Over half of the workforce is involved in the services. Most industry is 'light' – small factories producing lightweight goods. Bangladesh cannot afford to import raw materials needed for 'heavy' industries such as car- and ship-building.

At a brickworks outside Dhaka, firewood is used to fuel kilns in which the raw bricks are baked. ▼

🌐 Web Search ►►

► http://www.virtual bangladesh.com/ economy/index.html
Brief survey of Bangladeshi industry.

► http://www.bbsgov.org/
Data on employment by industry provided by Bangladeshi Bureau of Statistics.

► http://www.discoveryban gladesh.com/meetbangla desh/economy.html
Links to energy and labour information.

Transport

Biman, the Bangladesh national airline, has flights to 29 cities across Asia, Africa and Europe. There are also flights from the capital, Dhaka, to six other cities within Bangladesh. But most internal journeys are made by road, railway or waterway. Some 95 per cent of all the country's import and export freight passes through the seaports of Chittagong and Mongla.

More than 1,400 ships call at Chittagong harbour every year, loading and unloading 15 million tonnes of cargo. Mongla, in the Khulna region in the west, handles over 300 ships and 5 million tonnes of cargo a year. Bangladesh has a merchant fleet of around 30 ships, including bulk carriers, cargo ships, container ships and oil tankers.

River ports are important for inland transport. Two-thirds of Bangladesh is a wetland crossed by rivers and streams, and about 10 per cent of the country can be reached only by water transport. During the monsoon season the waterway network that is navigable by boats covers some 8,000 kilometres, but during the dry season this shrinks to 5,000 kilometres.

Road and rail networks

Most Bangladeshis live within 5 kilometres of a surfaced road. In 50 years, the total length of paved roads has increased from some 500 kilometres to nearly 20,000 kilometres. Today, more than 70 per cent of passengers and freight in Bangladesh goes by road. Private and state-owned bus services operate all over the country.

About a third of Bangladesh is covered by a railway network. Bangladesh Railway, which is state-owned, runs rolling stock that includes some 300 locomotives, 1,200 passenger coaches and 16,000 freight wagons between more than 500 stations.

Bicycles and Rickshaws

Forty per cent of all journeys in Dhaka are made by bicycle. There are few places in the world where the bicycle is used as extensively as it is here. Dhaka has more than 600,000 bicycle rickshaws – colourfully decorated passenger vehicles that are driven by pedal power. These are used by local people but are also popular with tourists. So too are the autorickshaws, which are similar but are motorized, and therefore quicker.

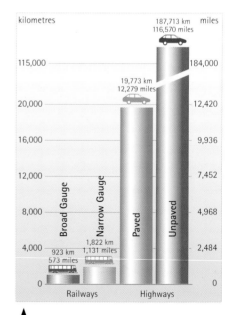

Comparison of the length of the rail and road networks.

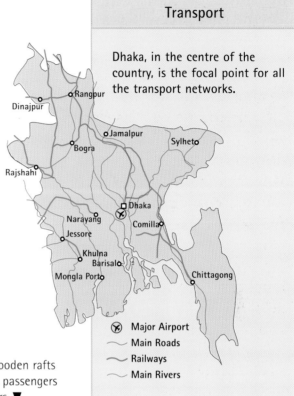

Transport

Dhaka, in the centre of the country, is the focal point for all the transport networks.

Rangpur
Dinajpur
Jamalpur
Bogra
Sylhet
Rajshahi
Dhaka
Narayang
Comilla
Jessore
Khulna
Barisal
Mongla Port
Chittagong

 Major Airport
Main Roads
Railways
Main Rivers

▲ Mainline trains are of standard size, as seen here in Dhaka. In many rural areas, small, narrow-gauge trains are used.

In rural areas, simple wooden rafts are used to ferry goods, passengers and vehicles across rivers. ▼

Web Search ►►

► http://www.bbsgov.org/
Data on railway rolling stock, water transport vessels and road vehicles.

► http://www.bimanair.com/
Website of Biman, the national airline of Bangladesh.

► http://www.discoverybangladesh.com/transportation.html
Information and statistics on Bangladesh's transport system.

Education

Bangladeshi children attend primary school for five years, between the ages of 6 and 11. Some then go on to secondary school and sit the School Certificate examination after a further five years. A few continue for two more years to gain their Higher School Certificate. Some of these then enter university.

Primary school attendance is compulsory and free of charge. Children study Bangla, English literature and, from Grade 3 (the third year), science. They are also taught life-skills for coping outside the classroom. There is an average of 59 pupils for every teacher. The school year is 37 weeks long. Some children, especially in rural areas, do not complete their primary education.

Secondary education is not generally free, and some secondary schools are privately owned. But the government pays for girls from rural areas to attend secondary school to encourage them to continue learning rather than get married at a young age. The thousand or so secondary schools in cities have the best facilities, with science laboratories and libraries. Often, rural schools have little scientific equipment, few science teachers and few books. Many children in rural areas do not attend secondary school.

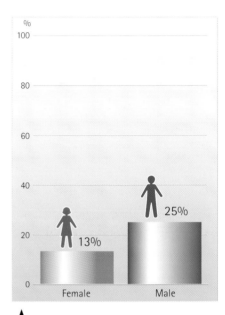

▲ Comparison of the percentage of males and females that go on to secondary education.

A classroom in a village school. In many rural schools, children of different ages are taught in the same class. ►►

18

Religious and university education

Some primary and secondary schools are religious schools called *madrasas*. There, the religion Islam is taught as well as the other subjects. Usually, the madrasa is attached to the local mosque, the house of worship for Muslims, the followers of Islam.

Secondary school pupils wishing to study for the Higher School Certificate must first pass the School Certificate examination. The higher qualification is needed to enrol for a degree course at a university or institute of technology. The University of Dhaka is the largest in Bangladesh.

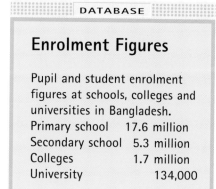

DATABASE

Enrolment Figures

Pupil and student enrolment figures at schools, colleges and universities in Bangladesh.

Primary school	17.6 million
Secondary school	5.3 million
Colleges	1.7 million
University	134,000

In secondary schools, young women are taught such household skills as embroidery and making clothes. ▼

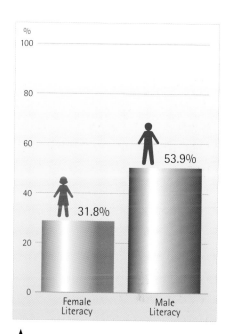

▲ There is a large difference in the percentage of women and men who can read and write.

Web Search ►►

► http://www.unicef.org/infobycountry/bangladesh_statistics.html
UNESCO International Bureau of Education survey and appraisal of education in Bangladesh.

► http://www.unicef.org/girlseducation/index.html
Summary of girls' education worldwide.

Sport and Leisure

Altogether, 27 internationally recognized sports are played in Bangladesh. Cricket, hockey and football are the most popular and are enjoyed by players and spectators alike. Kabbadi – a game a little like rugby, but without the ball – is the traditional, national sport.

Kabbadi is believed to be nearly 4,000 years old. It began as a way of developing self-defence skills among unarmed people, and may have originated in India. Poorer people in rural areas can and do enjoy kabbadi, as no equipment is needed, just an area of flat ground to play on.

Another traditional sport is boat racing. Every year, on rivers and canals across the country, teams of villagers race against each other in colourfully decorated rowing boats, accompanied by drum beats and the ringing of bells.

Children practise their footballing skills watched by their teacher. Football is played in parks, on school playing fields and on waste ground of convenient size. ▼

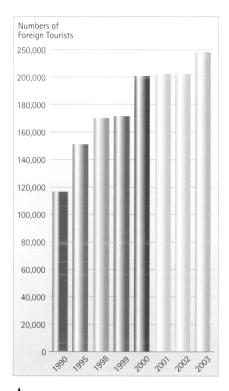

 The number of tourists visiting Bangladesh has nearly doubled in 10 years. Some come to watch such international sporting events as cricket and hockey.

 At a school sports gala, students perform a martial arts display. Traditional sports are a blend of activities from northern India, Myanmar and Tibet.

Playing and watching sports

In 1997, Bangladesh was recognized by the international Cricket Council as a One-Day International side, and three years later as a fully-fledged Test Match side. In 1999, the national team scored an historic victory in a one-day match against a very experienced Pakistan side.

Bangladesh also made history in chess by producing the first Grandmaster from the Indian subcontinent, after Niaz Murshed was awarded the title in 1986.

There are two international sports stadiums in Bangladesh, at Dhaka and Chittagong. Some 30 National Sports Federations run cricket, football, hockey, badminton, tennis, volleyball, basketball, boxing, cycling and other sports through district sports associations across the country. Women have a separate sports federation and their own sports complex, at Dhanmondi, in Dhaka.

Web Search ►►

► http://www.bssnews. net/about_sports_& _games.php

National News Agency of Bangladesh. Good overview of sports and history of sport in Bangladesh.

► http://www.bangla football.com/

Football news from Bangladesh, with web links to Manchester United, A.C. Milan and Diego Maradona among others.

Daily Life and Religion

Bangladesh has a larger Muslim population than most other countries. The nation's health and welfare services are improving and people are living longer. But wages are low and consumer goods, such as televisions, are expensive.

The vast majority of Bangladeshis are Muslims, followers of the religion of Islam. Other religious groups include Hindus, Buddhists and Christians. Hindus are evenly distributed across the country. Many of the tribes living in the Chittagong Hills are Buddhists.

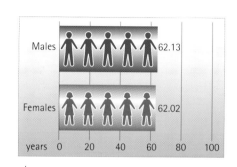

▲ In Bangladesh, men, on average, now live very slightly longer than women. Life expectancy for both sexes has risen by about 5 years in the last decade.

Wages, health and poverty

Poverty is a major problem, affecting more than one-third of the population. On average, people in Bangladesh earn the equivalent of around £240 a year. A television costs about four months' wages, and only some 0.4 per cent of the people have one. To buy a second-hand car would take more than 20 years' savings for someone on an average wage.

Health care is improving, with 70 per cent of children now being immunized against diseases such as polio and diphtheria, compared with 55 per cent some 10 years ago. There is, on average, about 1 doctor for every 4,500 or so patients.

Welfare services are gradually being developed to help disabled people, senior citizens, the unemployed and other disadvantaged groups.

A street trader in Dhaka. Most people buy food, clothes and household goods from market stalls and small shops. ▶▶

Armed Forces

Bangladesh has no military conscription. Service in the army, navy, air force or other branch of the armed forces, such as the Bangladesh Rifles, is voluntary. The armed forces not only have a duty to defend the country, but they also assist in times of natural disasters and serve as peace-keeping forces abroad for the United Nations. Armed forces personnel, who are mostly men, number about 125,000.

▲
▲ A Buddhist temple in a village in Chittagong. Buddhism, like Hinduism, came to the Bangladesh region long ago from India.

About 117 million Bangladeshis are Muslims. Hindus number around 15 million. There are fewer than 1 million each of Buddhists and Christians. Most Christians are Roman Catholics. ►►

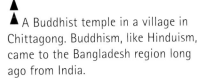

1%

11%

88%

■ Muslim   ■ Hindu

■ Buddhist, Christian and Other

The Working Week

Some factories run 24 hours a day, with workers operating in shifts. Shops and offices open between 9.00 a.m. and 5.00 p.m. from Saturday to Wednesday, and also on Thursday mornings. Sunday is a normal working day, and Friday is a day off for Muslim worship.

 Web Search ►►

► http://www.bangladesh army.info/
Official website of the Bangladesh Army, with information on recruitment, history of the armed forces and so on.

Arts and Media

The different cultures that have taken root over the centuries have given Bangladesh a rich and varied artistic tradition. This is reflected in its art, architecture, dance, drama, music, painting and poetry.

Examples of ancient Bangladeshi art include the terracotta reliefs, depicting village life, on the walls of the magnificent Buddhist monastery ruins at Paharpur in the south. An artistic achievement of modern times is the series of sketches of scenes of the great Bengal famine of 1943 by the painter Zainul Abedin.

The most famous Bengali writer is Rabindranath Tagore (1861–1941), who won the Nobel Prize for Literature in 1913. Tagore wrote poetry in the Bengali language, continuing a tradition that began more than 1,000 years ago.

Cinema

The first, full-length Bangladeshi feature film was made in 1956. Today, the country's film industry turns out about 60 films a year. *The Clay Bird*, a film directed by Tareque Masud and released in 2003, won widespread praise. The film tells the story of boy growing up in Bangladesh in the 1960s against the background of the coming war for independence.

Posters for a Bangladeshi film outside a cinema in Dhaka. Foreign films are usually shown with Bangla subtitles. ▼

Music, the press and broadcasting

Tradition runs strong through Bangladeshi music, dance and drama. Folk songs in the styles called *jari* and *shari* are sung to the accompaniment of traditional instruments, such as the *banshi* (bamboo flute) and *eklara* (a single-stringed lute), while both men and women perform a dance to the music.

About 200 daily newspapers are published in Bangladesh, 13 of them in English and the rest in Bangla. The English-language newspapers include the *Bangladesh Observer*, *Daily Star*, *Independent*, *Financial Express* and others. The total circulation is low compared with the number of people who can read: an average of only one copy for every 55 literate persons.

Some 75 per cent of people have access to a radio and about 60 per cent to a television. Betar (Radio Bangladesh) and BTV (Bangladesh Television) are stations run by the government, but there is also a choice of commercial and satellite stations.

▲ A woman performs a dance that combines local Bengali traditions and Hindu mythology.

🌐 **Web Search** ►►

► http://www.comminit.
com/st2002/sld-
5482.html
Information on Bangladesh print and broadcasting media.

► http://www.discovery
bangladesh.com/meet
bangladesh/art.html
Pages on literature, art, music, dance and drama.

Total numbers of television and radio broadcast stations. ▼
▼

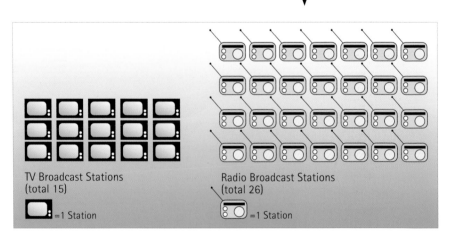

TV Broadcast Stations
(total 15)

☐ =1 Station

Radio Broadcast Stations
(total 26)

📻 =1 Station

Government

Tax

The government raises money to carry out its policies through taxation. Most of the tax comes from customs duties on imported goods. Value added tax is charged on many products at the manufacturing stage, but not on goods bought in shops. Anyone earning 225,000 takas (£2,410) or more a year pays between 10 and 25 per cent in income tax.

The People's Republic of Bangladesh is a parliamentary democracy. Elected members of Parliament, headed by a prime minister, govern the country. The official head of state is the president, but presidential duties are largely ceremonial. A written constitution guarantees the rights and freedoms of the Bangladeshi people.

The president is elected by Parliament (called the Jatiya Sangsad, or House of Nations) to serve for five years. Any candidate – man or woman – standing for president must have reached the age of 35. Parliament is made up of 300 members each of whom is elected by the people of his or her own electoral area. Parliamentary candidates, who usually represent one or other of the political parties, must

Provinces and Territories

The country is divided into six main administrative areas, called divisions or provinces. These are further broken down into districts, or *zilas*.

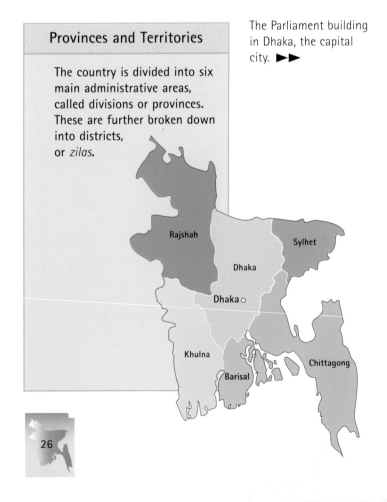

The Parliament building in Dhaka, the capital city. ▶▶

be at least 25. Voting is open to Bangladeshi citizens from the age of 18. The party that gains the most seats in the election forms the government and their leader, with the president's approval, becomes the prime minister.

A government may be in office for a maximum of five years, after which parliament is dissolved and fresh elections are held.

Political parties and freedom

The main political parties are the Awami League, Bangladesh National Party (BNP), Jamaat-i-Islami, Jatiya Party (Ershad faction), Jatiya Party (Naziur faction), Isla Oikya Jote and the Bangladesh Communist Party.

The state religion of Bangladesh is Islam but, under the constitution, Muslims must not be favoured in any way over followers of other religions. The constitution also states that men and women must be treated equally, there should be a free press, and everyone should be allowed freedom of speech.

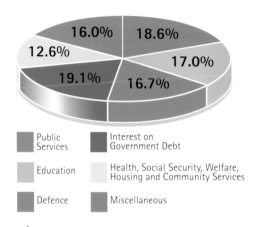

■ Public Services	■ Interest on Government Debt
■ Education	■ Health, Social Security, Welfare, Housing and Community Services
■ Defence	■ Miscellaneous

▲ The largest shares of government spending are allocated to public services and interest payable on loans at home and abroad. Expenditure on defence and education are also high priorities. 'Miscellaneous' includes public transport.

Web Search ►►

► http://www.bangladesh. net/article_bangladesh/ economic_trends/eco_ 14_bd_public_finance. htm
Review of Bangladesh public finance and discussion of budget.

► http://www.nbr-bd. org/
Website of the Bangladesh National Board of Revenue, giving details of income tax, VAT, customs duties and so on.

► http://www.bangladesh gov.org/
Bangladesh constitution website, giving the full text of the country's constitution.

Place in the World

Chronology of Historical Events: to 1974

500 BC
Tribal people establish kingdom of Vanga (Bengal)

AD750–1200
Rule by Buddhist Pala and Hindu Senha dynasties

1576
Conquered by Muslim Mughul emperor Akbar

1757
Defeat of last Muslim ruler, Nawab of Bengal, by the British, who become the new rulers of the Indian subcontinent

1947
British leave and partition subcontinent into India (Hindu) and Pakistan (Muslim). East Bengal becomes part of Pakistan, but with India in between

1949
Bangabandhu Sheikh Mujibur-Rahman ('Mujib') forms Awami League (AL), a political party calling for greater autonomy for East Bengal

1952
Student-led campaign launched 21 February 1952 for Bangla to be a state language of Pakistan alongside Urdu is put down by force

1970
Awami League wins all East Pakistani seats in elections to National Assembly

1971
National Assembly suspended and Sheikh Mujib arrested. Bengali nationalists proclaim independent republic of Bangladesh, and civil war follows. West Pakistan armies defeated with help from India

1972
First government of People's Republic of Bangladesh, with Sheikh Mujibur-Rahman as prime minister

The People's Republic of Bangladesh was born in war and revolution in 1971. Today, it is relatively politically stable, and a parliamentary democracy.

For nearly 200 years, the land that is today Bangladesh was, like the rest of the Indian subcontinent, ruled by Britain as part of its colonial empire. In 1947, when the British finally left, the subcontinent was split into two countries along religious lines. India was to be mainly for Hindus, and Pakistan for Muslims.

Because of the religious divide, India's eastern border cut the Bengal region in two. West Bengal was in India, but East Bengal belonged to Pakistan, which lay more than 1,500 kilometres to the west, on the other side of India. Inevitably, this led to confusion and conflict.

The High Court in Dhaka, the centre of the country's legal system. ▼

Independence and beyond

In March 1971, East Pakistan, as East Bengal was renamed, declared itself an independent republic called Bangladesh, and was attacked by the West Pakistan army. After a bitter civil war in which about three million people died, the first government of the new, independent republic of Bangladesh was formed in Dhaka in 1972.

Two years later, Bangladesh joined the United Nations (UN). Bangladesh also belongs to the Commonwealth of Nations, along with other former members of the British Empire, and is a founder member of the South Asian Association for Regional Cooperation (SAARC), whose stated aim is 'to accelerate the process of economic and social development in member states'.

Over 10 years, Bangladesh's economic performance and wealth increased by 51.6 per cent. By 2010, the country aims to halve the number of its poor people, which stands at around 45 million. To achieve this target, its economy will need to grow by a further 48 per cent – a big challenge.

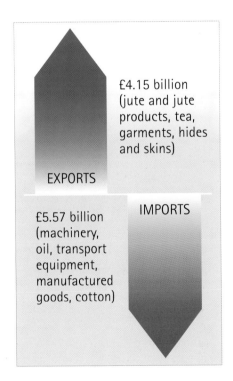

EXPORTS
£4.15 billion (jute and jute products, tea, garments, hides and skins)

IMPORTS
£5.57 billion (machinery, oil, transport equipment, manufactured goods, cotton)

◄◄ Bangladesh has a trade deficit – the value of its exports is less than the value of its imports.

Web Search ►►

► http://www.geographyiq.com/countries/bg/Bangladesh_history_summary.htm
Detailed history of the Bangladesh region from the time of the Mughul empire onward.

► http://www.worldbank.org/bd
World Bank website with economic and other data on Bangladesh.

Area:
147,570 sq km

Population size:
144,319,628

Capital city:
Dhaka (population 9,373,000)

Other major cities:
Chittagong (3,651,000), Khulna (1,442,000), Rajshahi (1,000,500), Gazipur (670,200), Narayaganj (382,600)

Longest river:
Ganges–Padma (part of Ganges) (306 km)

Highest mountain:
Tahjindong (1,412 m)

Currency:
Taka (Tk)

Flag:
The flag was adopted after independence as the national flag of the People's Republic of Bangladesh. The red disc, slightly off-centre, represents the sun of freedom and the blood that was shed to achieve independence. The green background represents the Bangladeshi countryside and is the traditional colour of Islam.

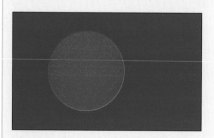

Languages:
Official language: Bangla (Bengali)

Natural resources
Natural gas, coal, lignite, peat, a little oil, limestone, sand, ceramic clay, hard rock, jute, bamboo

Major exports:
Ready-made clothes, jute and jute goods, tea, leather and leather goods, newsprint (paper for newspapers), fish, frozen foods

Some holidays and festivals
1 January: New Year's Day.
21 February: Shaheed Dibosh (Mourning Day). Honours four martyrs who lost their lives in 1952 when a demonstration to make Bangla a national language was fired on by police.
Early March (11th lunar month): Pawhela Falgun. 'First Day of Spring' when people attend fairs, exchange greetings, flowers, cards and gifts.
26 March: Independence Day. Anniversary of the declaration of independence from Pakistan made in 1971.
Mid-April (1st day, 1st lunar month): Pawhela Boishakh (Bengali New Year). Singing, processions and fairs to mark the beginning of the Bengali New Year.
15 August: Anniversary of the assassination, in 1975, of Sheikh Mujibur Rahman, who is considered to be the father of the Bangladesh nation.

Official religion:
Islam

Other religions
Hindu 11 per cent, Buddhist and Christian 0.9 per cent, others 0.1 per cent

3   2002   01430   6759

Glossary

BUDDHISM
Religion based on the teachings of Siddhartha Gautama, also known as the Buddha, or Enlightened One, who was born in north-eastern India in 563 BC.

COMMONWEALTH (OF NATIONS)
Association of independent countries, nearly all of which once belonged to the British Empire. They share a commitment to promote human rights, democracy and economic development.

CONSTITUTION
A list of principles, drawn up by the state, that sets out the powers and duties of the government and the rights, responsibilities and freedoms of the people.

CYCLONE
A region of very low pressure circled by a wind which, in tropical countries, often causes violent rainstorms.

DELTA
Sand and silt dumped by a river on the plain, near a river mouth, where the river slows and the main channel fans out into many smaller channels as the river reaches the sea.

DEMOCRACY
System of government in which representatives of political parties are freely elected by the people to form the government for a fixed period.

ETHNIC
Referring to the common racial, national, cultural or religious identity of a group of people.

FLOODPLAIN
Flat area crossed by a river some or all of which gets flooded when the river bursts its banks. It is made up of silt and soil deposited by the river.

GROSS DOMESTIC PRODUCT (GDP)
The value of all the goods and services produced by a country measured over a year or other period. Generally, the lower the GDP, the poorer the country.

HINDUISM
A 4,000-year-old religion that began in India, and is the major religion of India. Hindus worship many different gods and goddesses.

HYDRO-ELECTRIC POWER
Electrical power derived from flowing water, such as a river that has been dammed to provide energy for an electricity generator in a power station.

ISLAM
Religion begun by Muhammad, the Prophet, in AD622 in what is today Saudi Arabia. The name means 'submit', as to the will of God, and followers are called Muslims.

JUTE
A woody herb and its fibres, grown in river valleys and used to make string, matting, carpets, sacking and other products.

MANGROVES
Leafy tropical trees that grow in shallow, salty water near the coast and produce limb-like roots showing above the water line.

MONSOON
A wind that brings moisture from the sea and deposits it on the land as rain in the summer months. In winter, the monsoon blows in the opposite direction, from land to sea.

REPUBLIC
A country whose leaders are elected to govern, as opposed to, for example, a monarchy, where the power to rule is handed down through generations.

SILT
Very finely grained rocky material, containing little or no clay, that is dumped by slow-flowing rivers.

SUBCONTINENT
A large land mass, made up of several countries, such as India, Pakistan and Bangladesh, but smaller than the whole continent, in this case, Asia.

WORLD BANK
International organization, attached to the United Nations, that makes loans to governments for irrigation, education, housing and other projects.

Index